Land Warfare

By Martin J. Dougherty

Please visit our Web site www.garethstevens.com. For a free color catalog of all our high-quality books, call toll free 1-800-542-2595 or fax 1-877-542-2596.

Library of Congress Cataloging-in-Publication Data

Dougherty, Martin J.
    Land warfare / by Martin J. Dougherty.
        p. cm. _ (Modern warfare)
    Includes bibliographical references and index.
    ISBN-10: 1-4339-2727-6 ISBN-13: 978-1-4339-2727-0 (lib. bdg.)
    1. Military art and science_Juvenile literature. 2. Military history_Juvenile literature. I. Title.
U106.D68   2010
355.4_dc22
                                                      2009019090

This North American edition first published in 2010 by
Gareth Stevens Publishing
111 East 14th Street, Suite 349
New York, NY 10003

Copyright © 2010 by Amber Books, Ltd.
Produced by Amber Books Ltd., Bradley's Close
74–77 White Lion Street
London N1 9PF, U.K.

Amber Project Editor: James Bennett
Amber Copy Editors: Melanie Gray, Jim Mezzanotte
Amber Designer: Andrew Easton
Amber Picture Research: Terry Forshaw, Natascha Spargo

Gareth Stevens Executive Managing Editor: Lisa M. Herrington
Gareth Stevens Editor: Joann Jovinelly
Gareth Stevens Senior Designer: Keith Plechaty

Interior Images
BAE Systems: 16
Corbis: 24 (Russell Boyce/Reuters)
First Joint Public Affairs Unit, Australia: 13
Military Visualizations, Inc.: 1, 9, 15
U.S. Department of Defense: 3 (U.S. Navy), 4, 5, 6 (U.S. Marine Corps), 7, 8 (U.S. Air Force), 10, 11 (U.S. Marine Corps), 12 (U.S. Marine Corps), 14 (U.S. Air Force), 17, 18 (U.S. Army), 19 (U.S. Marine Corps), 20 (U.S. Air Force), 21, 22 (U.S. Army), 23 (U.S. Army), 25 (U.S. Army), 26, 27, 28, 29

Cover Images
Front cover: U.S. Department of Defense

Printed in the United States of America

CPSIA compliance information: Batch #CW10GS: For further information contact Gareth Stevens, New York, New York at 1-800-542-2595.

1 2 3 4 5 6 7 8 9 13 12 11 10 09

▶ DESERT LANDING
A U.S. Army Soldier watches a CH-53 helicopter land in Djibouti, Africa.

CONTENTS

CHAPTER 1

FIGHTING ON LAND

Battles can be fought in many places. They might be fought in the air or they might be fought at sea. However, most battles take place on land.

An army is a land force. It has many groups. One group is the **infantry**. They are the soldiers on the ground. Another group fires huge guns called **artillery**. Some groups drive tanks. Others transport food and other supplies.

Leading the Troops

Officers are the soldiers in charge. The top officers are generals. They have the highest

▼ TEAMWORK
Infantry soldiers from Romania, Bulgaria, and the United States are on a training mission so they can learn to work together as a team.

DID YOU KNOW?
Soldiers salute officers as a form of respect. The salute started long ago, when knights wore helmets. They flicked up their visors to speak to commanders.

◀ MARINE LEADER
A U.S. Marine Corps general inspects soldiers under his command. Soldiers must stand at attention with their arms by their sides when being inspected by a senior officer.

rank. They command large groups of soldiers. Officers with lower ranks lead smaller groups.

An officer leads **enlisted** soldiers. These soldiers carry out the orders. Some enlisted soldiers become leaders. They are called noncommissioned officers, or NCOs. Sergeants and corporals are NCOs.

Chain of Command

In most countries, the government tells the army to do a job, or mission. The generals plan how to do it. Then, they give orders. The orders get passed down to lower-ranked officers. They tell enlisted soldiers what to do.

This chain of command is important. Soldiers do dangerous jobs. They must follow orders. If they do not, someone might get hurt or killed.

Front Lines

Most top officers do not go into battle. Instead, they stay far from the front line. They give orders to lower-ranked officers, such as captains and lieutenants. Those junior officers lead troops into combat.

The top officers plan a mission. But even the best plan can go wrong. If it does, junior officers must decide what to do. They must come up with a new plan quickly. Lives may depend on it!

Keeping Contact

Soldiers must communicate. Top officers need to give orders. They also need to know what happens at the front line.

▼ DIRECTING THE ATTACK
U.S. Marines practice how to work with aircraft to bomb targets. They are telling bombers to attack a dummy, or fake, enemy position.

The signaller carries the radio. He stays close to the officer.

The officer uses the radio to tell the bombers exactly where to strike.

For years, soldiers have used radios and phones to send messages. Today, they also use laptop computers to send and receive information. They go to a special web site on the Internet. It gives them important information and updates.

Enemy Plans

For a plan to work, everyone needs to know it. But not the enemy! Soldiers try to learn what the other side is doing. They use spy **satellites**, or unmanned planes. Sometimes soldiers sneak into enemy territory.

Soldiers try to ruin plans, too. They may jam the enemy's radios, so top officers cannot talk to their troops. Then, if communication is disrupted, the chain of command helps maintain control. Soldiers still follow the same orders, but those directions come instead from junior officers.

▼ SPY IN THE SKY

This U.S. remote-controlled plane is called an Unmanned Aerial Vehicle (UAV). It can fly over the battle area. If it is shot down by the enemy, nobody gets hurt. The UAV's cameras let commanders see what is happening below.

CHAPTER 2

INFANTRY

Over the years, armies have changed in many ways. But one thing has always stayed the same: Infantry are foot soldiers. They fight on the ground. They have tough jobs!

Infantry are divided into groups. In the U.S. Army, a small group is a squad. It is about ten soldiers. Two to four squads make a platoon. A really large group is a brigade. It has more than 3,000 soldiers.

DID YOU KNOW?
A division can have more than 10,000 soldiers. The oldest U.S. division is the 1st, nicknamed "The Big Red One" or "The Fighting First." It has been around since World War I (1914–1918).

▼ ON HIGH ALERT
U.S. soldiers exit an armored personnel carrier (APC) in Iraq. They must watch all around for enemies.

Most U.S. troops use the M4A1 rifle. It is light and easy to handle. It can fire single shots, or many bullets quickly, like a machine gun.

The M4A1 has a handle to make it easy to carry. The rear sight is also built into the handle.

The sights on an M4A1 allow a skilled soldier to hit a target up to 1,600 feet (500 meters) away. When the front sight is lined up with the rear sight, the rifle is pointing straight at its target.

The end of the barrel is called the **muzzle**. The slots on the tip help stop muzzle **flash** from blinding soldiers when they shoot.

The **magazine** holds 30 rounds of ammunition. That's a lot of firepower! When the magazine is empty, the soldier takes it out and puts in a full one.

The **stock** of the rifle fits tightly against a person's shoulder so it stays steady when shooting.

Getting Around

In the past, infantry walked to war. Even if they walked quickly, travel was slow. Today, infantry still **march**. But they have other ways to get around, too.

Today's soldiers ride in special trucks. They are called armored personnel carriers, or APCs. Those trucks protect them from attack. Soldiers jump from planes with parachutes. They use helicopters. They also ride on boats.

DID YOU KNOW?

Some soldiers are in **mechanized infantry**. Unlike "light" infantry, they do not fight on foot. Instead they ride in APCs and other armored vehicles. They can get to destinations quickly and strike with force.

Infantry Equipment

Good boots are important to infantry, as are clothes that keep soldiers warm and dry. They also need protection during combat. They wear helmets and **body armor**.

Infantry carry everything they need. Soldiers carry food, called **rations**. They carry sleeping bags and other equipment. Infantry also carry weapons. They must move quickly, even with heavy loads.

▼ **IN THE FIELD**

These U.S. soldiers are fighting terrorists in Afghanistan. Most infantry soldiers use rifles. But some carry more powerful machine guns to support their squad.

This soldier uses a M240E machine gun that rests on a tripod.

Helmets and uniforms are **camouflaged**. Strips of material made to look like plants disguise the helmet. Enemies cannot easily spot soldiers wearing camouflaged uniforms.

▼ ANTITANK
Infantry can fight tanks if they have the right weapons. These U.S. soldiers use a Javelin antitank missile launcher.

Infantry Weapons

Soldiers carry many weapons. Most carry rifles. Those rifles can fire single shots or they can shoot rapidly, like a machine gun. Soldiers put a knife on the end of the rifle, called a **bayonet**. Infantry carry hand **grenades**, too. They also carry weapons to fire at tanks.

In most infantry units, a soldier carries a machine gun. Another soldier may carry a grenade launcher. That weapon fires a grenade much farther than it can be thrown.

DID YOU KNOW?

A grenade launcher can hit a target 1,300 feet (400 m) away. Some machine guns can hit targets more than 1 mile (2 kilometers) away. They shoot almost 20 bullets a second.

11

Infantry in Training

Infantry get a lot of training. They face some hard tests. They go through obstacle courses. They run long distances with heavy loads. Soldiers also learn how to use weapons.

During training, soldiers go on exercises. An exercise is a pretend battle. Two sides "fight" each other, as if they were in combat. On those exercises, infantry learn to work together. They also learn how to work with tanks and artillery.

▼ TRAINING FOR THE REAL THING
U.S. Marines are trained to handle whatever happens in battle. These marines are taking part in a large training exercise. As they move forward, other soldiers and artillery gunners are ready to give them **covering fire**.

▲ AIRBORNE INFANTRY
Airborne infantry travel in aircraft. They get around faster than troops traveling on the ground. These soldiers are being carried into battle by helicopter.

Special Forces

A few soldiers join Special Forces. Those units are small teams. They are usually the best soldiers. They do the hardest, most dangerous jobs.

Special Forces rescue hostages, or they go into enemy territory. They carry out **surveillance** to learn what the enemy is doing. They undertake raids against targets that are hard to reach.

DID YOU KNOW?

Many countries have Special Forces. The U.S. Army's Special Forces are called the Green Berets. Those soldiers go through tough training that can take as long as two years to complete!

CHAPTER 3

TANKS

Tanks help win battles. They travel faster than infantry. They have big, powerful guns. Tanks are important weapons for most armies.

A tank must travel wherever it is needed. It can move across rough ground. It also has thick armor to protect the crew inside.

Tank Technology

A modern tank's armor is made from many layers of **ceramic**, plastic, steel, and other metals. It is very tough. It is only a few inches thick, but is as strong as 4 feet (1.2 meters) of solid steel. Armor is heavy, so tanks must have powerful engines.

▼ "THE STEEL FIST"
The M1A1 Abrams is a U.S. tank. It is one of the toughest in the world. For a tank, it can travel fast—more than 40 miles (64 km) per hour. It can destroy almost anything on the battlefield.

▼ THE M1A1 ABRAMS

The M1A1 Abrams is a main battle tank. This kind of tank has a large main gun and heavy armor. The gun can destroy buildings or other tanks from 2 miles (3.2 km) away, often with one shot.

The commander has a machine gun to defend the vehicle and crew.

The main gun has a **caliber** of 4.7 inches (120 millimeters). The caliber is the **diameter** of the space inside the barrel. Most guns are identified by their caliber.

Shells for the main gun are stored in the back of the **turret**.

Armored plates protect the **hull** and the tank's **tracks**. If one track is damaged a tank cannot move and could be hit by the enemy.

All tanks have a main body called the hull. It holds the engine and space for the crew. The turret sits on top. It can spin around, even when the tank does not move. It holds the main gun and smaller machine guns.

Tanks get around on tracks instead of wheels. They are long metal belts. There is one track on each side. They dig into the earth. With tracks, tanks can get across rough or muddy ground.

DID YOU KNOW?

You steer a car by turning the front wheels. A tank's tracks do not turn in the same way. Tanks turn only when a track on one side goes faster. Then the tank turns toward the slower side.

Tank Crews

All tanks have a driver who sits in the hull. The driver sees outside with a **periscope**. A gunner fires the weapons. Another soldier helps with other jobs.

A tank commander decides what the tank will do. The commander gives orders to the driver and gunner. Tank crews work together as a team in a tiny space.

Tank Versus Tank

The first tanks were used to attack infantry. Today, tanks mostly fight each other. Some tanks can be hit and keep going, but most cannot withstand a direct strike.

Tank crews try to stay protected. They hide the tank behind a wall or ridge.

▲ EUROPEAN ARMOR

The Challenger 2 is a British main battle tank. Snow and ice are no problem for the Challenger's big tracks. This tank costs about $8 million to build. The British Army has more than 400 Challenger 2 tanks.

IN THEIR OWN WORDS

"I was wounded three times in Iraq the last time I was there.... [In one incident] I took a sniper bullet, 7.62 mm, to the front of the helmet, straight in front, almost right between the eyes. I fell into the turret of the tank."

U.S. Army Staff Sgt. Matthew Sims

Only the turret peeks over the top. The hull bottom has less armor. To protect themselves, the crew tries to stay "hull-down." They make sure the hull is not a target.

▼ TANK COMMANDER
This U.S. Army tank commander is in the turret of an M60 tank. There is not much space to move around! The M60 is older than the M1A1 Abrams, but it is still used all over the world.

DID YOU KNOW?
The U.S. Army uses the M1 tank. In 1991, many M1s fought in the Gulf War. That tank uses a **gas turbine**. Jet planes also use this kind of engine.

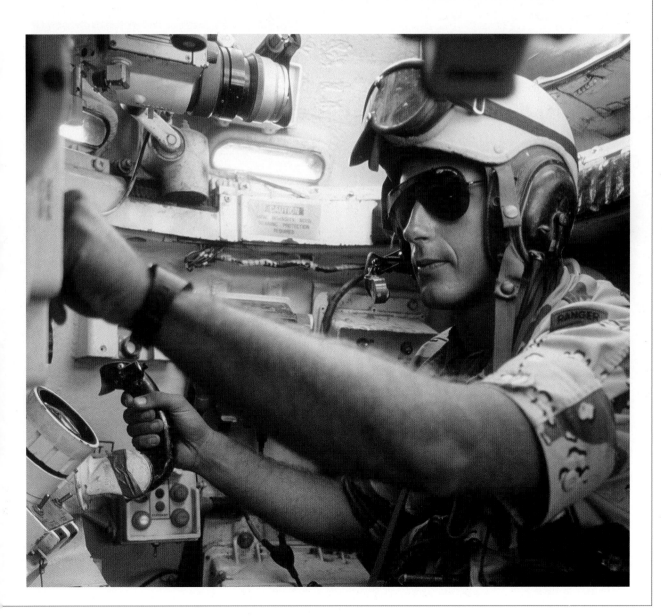

Tank Tactics

A tank's armor is thickest at the front. Commanders try to attack enemy tanks from the sides and rear. At the same time, they make sure their tank's front is facing the enemy.

Tank commanders must think quickly. A single hit could destroy the tank. They must always stay protected, but they also need to be able to fire their gun at the enemy. Once they hit a target, they move to another location.

DID YOU KNOW?

Today, some tanks have computers to help gunners aim. Tanks can hit a target that is 3 miles (5 km) away. The gun's **shell** takes about three seconds to reach its target.

▼ RUSSIAN POWER
Thousands of T-72 main battle tanks were built in Russia in the 1970s and 1980s. The inside of the T-72 is so small that only soldiers who are 5 feet 4 inches (1.6 m) or shorter can operate it!

This M1A1 Abrams tank fires its main gun. The explosives that send the shell out of the barrel make a cloud of flame. Some shells are more than 2 feet (60 centimeters) long and weigh 40 pounds (18 kilograms).

Antitank Weapons

During a battle, a tank is a large target. Vehicles and aircraft attack it with guided **missiles**. Infantry also carry weapons that can destroy a tank. Those are called light antitank weapons (LAWs). They can launch a single **rocket**.

LAWs are effective weapons. They can be directed to land on top of a tank where its armor is thinnest and most fragile. LAWs can also drop down on top of tanks by using parachutes before exploding!

Other tanks and antitank guns also attack tanks. They fire special shells that smash through armor. Ditches and obstacles can trap a tank, too. Mines can damage a tank's tracks, so it cannot move.

CHAPTER 4

ARTILLERY

Armies use artillery to hit distant targets. Artillery can be big guns that fire shells. It can also be rockets.

A piece of artillery fires a **payload**. It is what the shell or rocket carries. A payload can be an explosive. It blows up the target. A payload might be just smoke, so the enemy cannot see, or it can be land mines that fly in different directions.

Mortars and Howitzers

Mortars are short metal tubes. They fire shells high into the air. Mortars cannot hit targets that are far away, but they are light and easy to move. Infantry units often have a few light mortars.

DID YOU KNOW?

A group of artillery weapons is called a **battery**. The name comes from hundreds of years ago. Back then, soldiers used cannons to "batter" down castle walls.

▼ BIG AND LOUD
U.S. soldiers fire a 4.15-inch (105-mm) light **howitzer**. This gun might look huge, but it is small compared to some artillery weapons.

▲ AIR DEFENSE
This vehicle carries a six-barrel 0.78-inch (20-mm) cannon to shoot down enemy aircraft. Its gun can fire very fast. The vehicle takes it wherever it is needed.

A howitzer is larger than a mortar. It is heavier, too. It has a short barrel, but it can fire a shell farther than a mortar. Howitzers need bigger crews than mortars.

The Big Guns

Some artillery weapons are **self-propelled**. They move around on their own power. Other artillery get towed behind vehicles.

The biggest guns have huge, powerful shells. They can hit targets more than 50 miles (80 km) away. Special vehicles move them around and carry their heavy shells.

Rockets and Missiles

Armies also use rockets or missiles. Rockets cannot be controlled after they are fired. They may or may not hit their targets. Missiles can be guided to their targets by soldiers.

Soldiers often fire many rockets at once, to make sure that some hit the target. Missiles are usually fired one at a time.

▼ ARTILLERY ROCKETS

Some artillery systems fire rockets instead of shells. The U.S. Army uses a system called MLRS (Multiple-Launch Rocket System). It fires a lot of rockets quickly.

The launcher has a big rack that stores many rockets. It fires one or two rockets at a time, or all of them at once.

The launcher is mounted on a huge truck. The truck takes it wherever it is needed.

Becoming a Gunner

Firing artillery takes a lot of skill. Gunners learn to take care of their weapons, not just fire them. They handle shells that could explode. Their jobs must be done with great care.

Gunners learn to work with other forces. They help infantry and tanks by hitting enemy targets. Gunners go on exercises with other troops. They learn how to work as part of a team.

DID YOU KNOW?

Some howitzers are self-propelled. They have tracks instead of wheels. These guns look like tanks. They can aim and fire, then move away. Soldiers say these guns can "shoot and scoot."

Controlling the Guns

Gunners work with soldiers called spotters. The spotters stay ahead of the guns. They find targets. Then, they radio the gunners and tell them exactly where to shoot.

The spotters watch where the shells come down. If the shells miss, they tell gunners where to aim the next time. When the shells hit their target, the gunners keep firing until they destroy the target.

▼ **ARTILLERY SHELLS**
This U.S. Army soldier is getting another shell to load into his team's 6.1-inch (155-mm) M777 gun. The shells are kept away from the gun for safety.

CHAPTER 5

SUPPLYING SOLDIERS

Some soldiers do not fight. Instead, they bring supplies to other soldiers. That job is very important. Without supplies, armies are in danger of losing battles.

An army needs many supplies to keep fighting. It needs fuel and spare parts. It needs **ammunition**, such as bullets. An army also needs food and clothing for troops. Supplies must get to the right place at the right time. That job is called **logistics**.

Always Moving

Supplies must reach troops in combat. Trucks often bring the supplies. They move along supply routes. Enemies may try to attack the trucks, so soldiers must defend them.

When trucks cannot reach the battlefields, helicopters bring supplies. Planes may also drop supplies by parachute. Pilots must make sure the supplies do not land in the wrong place!

▼ ON THE MOVE
A group of trucks carrying supplies is called a **convoy**. Convoys are protected by combat vehicles or tanks.

Tracking Supplies

Logistics officers keep track of supplies. They are also called quartermasters. They figure out who needs what. Then, they make sure soldiers get what they need. Those soldiers have important jobs.

Today, most quartermasters use computers. The computer has a system that keeps track of all shipments. Quartermasters enter a code number. Supplies usually get delivered in a few days.

IN THEIR OWN WORDS

"As troops move forward, we set up distribution points just behind the lines.... But we can't send in an aid truck before the fighting is over.... It would get hit and innocent people would die."

British Army Sgt. Iain Menzies, quartermaster

Open Roads

Army engineers also help transport supplies. They make sure roads are open for supply trucks. They may fix roads, or keep them safe for traveling. They clear away roadblocks and mines. Engineers also build bridges. They make sure the trucks keep moving over water or rough land.

Engineers do not usually fight, but they have dangerous jobs, too. Enemy troops may try to stop them. Engineers may carry weapons. They also get protection from infantry and tanks.

DID YOU KNOW?

Quartermasters must be careful when reviewing requests for supplies. For example, a soldier in Germany tried to order some pants. But, he put the wrong code in the computer. He ordered a fighter jet instead!

Eating on the Go

The world has many different soldiers, but they all have one thing in common. They

▼ CLEARING THE WAY
Combat engineers use a special kind of tank to clear the road. It has a bulldozer blade to push aside dirt and rubble.

▲ PICNIC, ARMY STYLE
In the U.S. Army, rations are called MREs (Meals, Ready To Eat). Each MRE contains a main meal and a dessert. Popular meals include chicken fajitas, vegetarian burgers, and beef stew.

hate the food they eat! Rations are not like regular food. Soldiers have no place to cook, so rations must be pre-cooked. They must stay fresh for long periods. Soldiers have to carry them, so they must be small and light. Sometimes, soldiers eat the same food every day.

▼ LAND WARRIOR

Foot soldiers are equipped with very tough and specialized equipment. This U.S. Army platoon leader is on patrol in Iraq. Soldiers in most armies use similar clothing and equipment.

The soldier's helmet protects his head. It also has a holder for night-vision goggles. They enable the soldier to see in the dark.

The rifle is carried in a special harness. The soldier can get at it quickly.

Uniforms contain many pockets for rations, ammunition, and other important items.

Knee pads protect the soldier's knees when he has to kneel on rough ground or climb over obstacles.

Boots are light, tough, and waterproof. Good boots are very important to any soldier. It is hard to fight well if your feet hurt.

Wearing the Uniform

Soldiers wear different uniforms at different times. Dress uniforms are for special events. Combat uniforms are for working and fighting. Soldiers also have special uniforms for hot and cold weather, and for wearing when in training.

Badges are part of uniforms. They are called **insignia**. Soldiers wear different insignia depending on their jobs. Infantry and engineers wear specific insignia, as do tank and artillery crews.

DID YOU KNOW?

Service members must follow strict dress codes. The U.S. Army, Navy, Air Force, and Marines also have policies that set standards for personal grooming. Members must even obtain permission to wear certain sunglasses or other eyewear!

▼ BADGES AND INSIGNIA
These soldiers are part of the Green Berets, the U.S. Army Special Forces. Badges on their shoulders and arms show their rank and job. They also wear medals and awards on their chests.

GLOSSARY

ammunition—the objects that guns fire, such as bullets and shells

artillery—huge guns used by land forces that can fire shells great distances

battery—a group of artillery weapons

bayonet—a knife that is attached to the barrel of a rifle

body armor—special covering that soldiers wear to protect their bodies from enemy fire

caliber—the size of a gun barrel and the bullet or shell it fires

camouflaged—giving something the same shape or colors as its surroundings, so it blends in and is hard to see

ceramic—hard material made from fired clay

convoy—soldiers and vehicles traveling together in a group

covering fire—an attack by soldiers that lets other soldiers get closer to the enemy without being hit

diameter—measurement of a circle or cylinder. It is the length of a straight line that passes from one side to the other through the center.

enlisted—having joined the army without going to school to become an officer

flash—a short, sudden burst of bright light

front line—during battles, the place where soldiers are fighting the enemy

gas turbine—a kind of engine that uses burning gases to spin fan blades

grenades—small bombs that soldiers can throw, or can fire from grenade launchers

howitzer—a big gun that can fire large shells a great distance

hull—the main part of a tank that holds the crew and engine

infantry—soldiers who fight on land

insignia—markings on a uniform that show a soldier's rank

logistics—the job of getting food and equipment to soldiers

magazine—the part of a rifle or machine gun that holds the ammunition

march—to walk quickly at the same speed and in a formation

mechanized infantry—soldiers who use armored vehicles for traveling and fighting

missiles—rockets that fly to a target and explode

muzzle—the end of a rifle where the bullets shoot out

payload—the ammunition a large gun fires, or the explosives that a missile or bomb carries

periscope—a device used by submarines and tanks that lets people see things while remaining hidden

rank—the position of a soldier in the chain of command, with a general having the highest rank and a private having the lowest rank

rations—the food that soldiers carry and eat

rocket—a long tube filled with fuel that takes off into the air, traveling fast and far

satellites—spacecraft that orbit, or circle, Earth, and send down information

self-propelled—able to travel without being pulled by a vehicle

shell—the ammunition that a large gun fires

stock—the part of a rifle that fits against the body when a soldier fires

surveillance—a close watch on what the enemy is doing, without being seen

tracks—metal belts on each side of a tank that turn to make the tank move

turret—the top part of a tank that holds the main gun and can turn around

FOR MORE INFORMATION

Books

Encyclopedia of the U.S. Army. Alan Axelrod (Checkmark Books, 2006)

Green Berets in Action. Special Ops (series). Marc T. Nobleman (Bearport Publishing, 2008)

The M1 Abrams Main Battle Tank. Steve Parker (Capstone Press, 2007)

Self-Propelled Howitzers: M109A6 Paladins. Michael and Gladys Green (Edge Books, 2004)

Soldier. Eyewitness Books (series). Simon Adams (DK Publishing, 2009)

U.S. Army Infantry Fighting Vehicles. Blazers (series). Martha E. Rustad (Capstone Press, 2006)

Web Sites

First Cavalry Division Museum
www.first-team.us/journals/ftmuseum
Explore a virtual museum about the 1st Cavalry Division, an infantry division in the U.S. Army.

How Stuff Works: Bradley Fighting Vehicles
www.science.howstuffworks.com/bradley.htm
Learn more about the Bradley Fighting Vehicle that carries mechanized infantry into battles.

How Stuff Works: M1 Tanks
www.science.howstuffworks.com/m1-tank.htm
Learn more about the M1 tank and see detailed photos of it.

U.S. Army: A Year in Photos, 2008
www.army.mil/yearinphotos/2008
Review amazing photos of U.S. soldiers from around the world. You can see soldiers training for battles, giving aid to civilians, and jumping from planes!

U.S. Army Fact Files: Weapons Systems
www.army.mil/factfiles/index.html
Discover all kinds of weapons and other equipment used by the U.S. Army, including tanks, rifles, howitzers, and mortars.

INDEX

ABOUT THE AUTHOR

Martin J. Dougherty holds a Bachelor of Education degree from the University of Sunderland in the United Kingdom. He has taught throughout northeast England and his published work includes books on subjects as diverse as space exploration, martial arts, and military hardware. He is an expert on missile systems and low-intensity warfare.